Promises Kept

Overcoming Challenges Through A Spiritual Journey

Dr. Victor Frias

ISBN 978-0-7414-9974-5
eISBN 978-0-7414-9975-2

Printed in the United States of America

Published June 2014

INFINITY PUBLISHING
1094 New DeHaven Street, Suite 100
West Conshohocken, PA 19428-2713
Toll-free (877) BUY BOOK
Local Phone (610) 941-9999
Fax (610) 941-9959
Info@buybooksontheweb.com
www.buybooksontheweb.com

For Inez, the great teacher, healer, wise counsel -
you carefully molded your son to value the
quintessential essence of the moment

Contents

Part III

Dedication

I dedicate this book to Inez Frias who passed away from my life in the Summer of 2011. I would also like to present this story to my children, my son Federico, daughters Denphenie, Vanessa and, of course, Roman Alexander-my grandson. I thank you for listening and putting up with my stories and frustrations when it mattered most. You know what I mean guys. As I move into the second phase of my life, I wanted you to know *a little* about my past and why it was important to protect you. I realize that work and school made it impossible for me to always be there for you but God knows we delighted in quality time.

My brothers Mark and Leo, nephew Mark, nieces Briana, Nayaliz, Shalibel and sister Mari, thanks for your on-going presence, vote of confidence, support, love and motivation for me to pursue and fulfill my promise to Mom to complete this most endearing journey.

My dear friends Daniel, Annie, Cassandra, and Kym these past two years have been remarkable and life-changing (you know what I mean). Your love, listening and endearing advice have lifted my soul at times when things have been the most difficult. Finally, to those of you whose silence has meant much-it is because of this silence that today I stand proud, passionate and filled with conviction in faith. I run to you in Christ.

Acknowledgements

My most profound and sense of gratitude and respect go to Kitty Oliver and mentors who provided an insurmountable level of guidance and patience and spiritually inoculated my soul along the way. Dr. Drabik, you allowed me to fulfill a life-long promise and, for that, I will be eternally grateful. Dean Esa, you prayed and guided me along the way during moments in my life where I didn't believe this was possible. I am encouraged and see you as a role model for those of us who aspire to do mission work. Dr. Mullings, you have embodied the word mentor throughout this process. Your words of encouragement motivated and inspired me along the way. Dr. Bowe-Lee, what can I say? Your guidance, from start to finish paved the way for the realization of a dream. This dream began three years ago; your ongoing support strengthened me in times of great despair. You are my friend, colleague, and mentor, always.

To my friends who would often lean on me and push me to complete my undergraduate studies while working as a doorman in mid-town

Manhattan in New York City over twenty five years ago. Sidney Bernstein and Henrietta Barnes, your financial and moral support will be forever cherished. For the countless others who have contributed to my spiritual and educational maturity, I am thankful, in particular, to my pastors, graduate professors, Jason, Tommie, John, Elsie and Ed. Ed, I am only half the teacher you are; you are a master trainer and the master historian.

PART ONE

THE EARLY YEARS

Introduction

There are those of you out there who simply have had a difficult time trying to figure out how to get away from the past. School has become a bore. Your girlfriend has just told you that she is pregnant. Your mom is saying she can't send you any more money for college. You get discouraged and decide to get back to the city and find a job, but what skills do you have? How will you support your mom? What about your pregnant girlfriend? How about the time you were confronted by your dad when you got home late and got that belt right across your back? What about the day you had enough and ran away to sleep in the park for three days? There was no food or money. By the way, this wasn't new; you were homeless when you were five. I don't know about you but I think this guy needed some help. What do you think? How did he cope and what has become of him throughout these four decades? Who guided and motivated him along the way and where did he find courage to carry on?

I am writing to you because I think we have some things in common. I was able to gain that courage and freedom I was referring to about a year ago. This is a raw story about a homeless kid from the Dominican Republic who came to the States, survived countless educational barriers including dropping out at age 16, becoming a father at 20, and held three jobs, attended college full time on Saturday and Sundays while pursuing several graduate degrees.

I got that help from mentors, from scripture and from the most wonderful woman in the world - mom. I am writing to you because much of what I am and what I think is because she believed in me. She never gave up, and saw potential in me. This book fulfills my promise to her.

Chapter 1:

Overcoming Childhood Trauma at a Young Age

- Can you still recall an incident that happened to you as far back as four years old?
- What happened?
- Why is it that you still recall this experience, and what emotions are you feeling now?

Feelings of helplessness, despair, loneliness and depression. Experiences of chaos, disorder, confusion and separation. Memories of nightmares, arguments, callousness and enslavement. How can we get rid of these in our lives? Researchers have looked into this field for some time, and yet they have not found the seed that promotes "a lifelong solution."

The truth is, stuff happens every day, and it doesn't discriminate! Everyone encounters these issues to some degree. For many of us, however, the result is deeply-rooted emotions that cripple the very core of our spiritual identity. Trust me, I know. This is perhaps one of the most profound reasons why I am writing this book.

I am a success story by the standards of the world – an immigrant to the United States who has endured hardships and overcome. But, personally, I have also faced situations where I have often searched and cried out in utter desperation to get an answer, but could not find a "fix" to what I considered obstacles. Several years ago, I became aware of an unusual feeling, an emotional and spiritual awakening which I had only once before experienced when I was sixteen years old when I attended a church function in New York City.

The church did an re-enactment of the crucifixion of Christ. I was transported to a different dimension by what was depicted on the cross. It's an image I will forever treasure and hold as sacred in my heart. There was a sense of peace and a lifting of sadness in my heart - something I had never experienced. Why was I moved? I believed in God and was baptized as a Catholic. What was different this time? These became questions that I pondered for a long time.

The memory resurfaced twenty-one years later by what, today, I call a supernatural encounter with Christ Jesus that transformed my life. And now, five years later, I write my story from the perspective of a humble father, brother, uncle, friend, teacher, school administrator, counselor, and spiritual leader who wants you to know that you, too, can overcome.

I began life in struggle in the Dominican Republic - homeless at the age of about four, faced challenges as an immigrant child in the U.S. public school system and survived those challenges as a result of something – Someone - much bigger than I.

GROWING UP IN THE GHETTOS OF THE DOMINICAN REPUBLIC

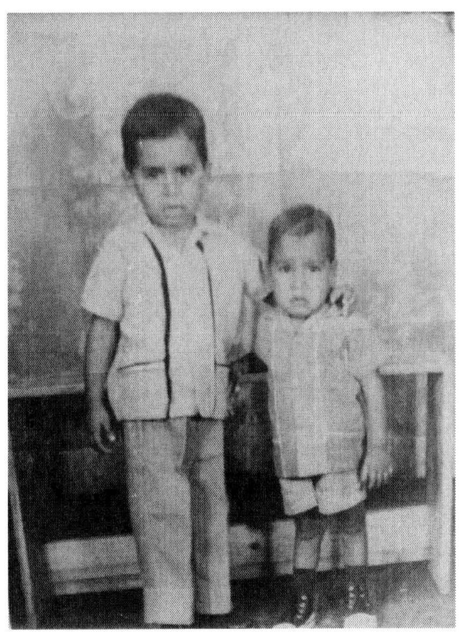

I grew up with my younger brothers Mark and Billy - who was born deaf and mute - in the ghettos of Bonao in the Dominican Republic. We would move so often, I can't even remember going to school until the age of eight when we moved to the United States.

For as long as I can remember, Mark and I were inseparable. I can recall as far back as the age of four, and Mark was three, when we would wander the streets looking for food. I remember collecting bottles and cardboard boxes, taking them to the local *el colmado* (grocery store) to get a piece of bread and some salami. Yes, that's how we fed ourselves.

Let me explain: My dad remarried, immigrated to the U.S., and left us behind in the Dominican

Republic with our biological mother. She was in her twenties, uneducated and homeless. She was young and did her best to try to take care of us, but it was never enough. Strangers and neighbors would take us in simply because we were just too young. Sleeping en la tierra, on the floor, with a couple of bed sheets, was the norm for us. I can't remember sleeping in a normal bed until we got to the States.

Every time I would see an airplane flying overhead, I would remind Mark that one day we, too, would be up there. How did I overcome this feeling of despair and loneliness at such a young age? Well, I had hope and that was my initial experience with spirituality.

SURVIVING AND ON MY OWN

Mark and I would often sneak into church and listen to some of the sermons. I had no idea what the priest was talking about, but he always gave us something to eat!

Suffice it to say, Mark and I were partners. I could never stop looking out for him. At times, we were so hungry I would look for the next funeral. Yes, this is where we would get our next meal. Can you relate, or do you know someone who can?

Most Dominican households have lunch at noon, and all the leftovers are usually thrown out. During those early years I would often wait and go to the back of the kitchen to pick up these leftovers because they were all we had. The maids were angels; they often kept a plate for us "*Muchachos, tienen hambre y donde esta su mama*?" they would say, asking if we were hungry and where was our mother. Our answer was simple - at the bar with God knows whom.

It's difficult to express simply the long term impact of these experiences on Mark and me. The one thing I was certain about at that time was that one day I would be in the States. That's what my dad had promised.

I remember traveling to a farm one day and as we picked tomatoes for our meal I saw my mother pass by on the back of a motorcycle drinking rum, as usual. I rushed to get Mark and both of us ran as fast as we could towards her, waving, hoping she would see us. It never happened, and she just zoomed out of sight. Mark was inconsolable and we embraced for a while. Then I pulled him back into the field and we ate tomatoes all afternoon. You can imagine what type of damage that did to our stomachs. But at least I was somehow able to distract Mark and got him to play hide and seek.

You're probably saying to yourself right now, yeah, this was a tough moment. But how did you manage to cope with such an awful event? I held on to the hope that one day dad would make good on his promise and get us to the States. But, folks, it never happened. We were sent to an uncle at another farm. I'm not sure how old I was, but I do recall that Mark and I hashed out an escape route to get to mom and got caught-(*no agarro y nos amarro*). Our uncle caught us and tied us with twine under the kitchen table, on the dirt floor. How did we get out you ask? Well, it turns out my dad found out about the treatment and sent a cousin to get us back to Bonao. This was a turning point for us. You see, dad had started the process to get us visas to travel to the States in 1972. I was four years old.

Mark and I have our differing opinions about this experience. As bitter as it was, it happened. I coped, collecting these emotions and hiding them so far in the back of my mind that all I could think about was when am I ever going to go to school? Going to school as a kid was not the type of conversation my mom and I had (so what - I was only eight). I saw other kids going to school; why couldn't we attend as well? But, we were too busy moving around and unable to pay the rent. That's the reason why we traveled at night.

HOPE

There were countless times I remember my mother bringing strangers into the house. Yes, that's what was going on. I have forgiven her, but it doesn't mean that I wasn't scarred.

However, despite these early challenges in my life, I held on to hope. Hope is the essence that drives and prompts your soul to be moved out of that dark place of restlessness and sadness. I will agree with you that memories such as these can lead to a crippled life, but I trusted in something far superior to me, call it divine "whispers." I just knew that I could not give up on a dream of meeting my dad in the States. This was the one constant that rooted me, that remained in me and crafted my survival during the most difficult of times. I guess this was one of those experiences that shaped my mindset and ability to cope early on. Once we arrived in the States, we had stability.

Chapter 2:

Stability and Personal Growth

- What are the thoughts that stimulate a person's heart, mind and soul?
- Can we get rid of the temptations of everyday living?
- What are the deeply rooted problems that continue to hurt us?

Some people go to the doctor to deal with their obstacles; others go to their spiritual leader; while others confide in a friend. You have the will power to go right to The Source that has supplied inspiration from the very beginning of time, to countless generations, but it is a decision that only you make for yourself.

I have learned that there is an overwhelming Presence filled with strength and majesty, holding all things together from inception. Even when we break away from the Source that brings meaning and substance in life, there remains an invisible bridge that links us back to the one thing that created us. Understanding this connection and alignment to grace and Presence of the Lord takes time, devotion and obedience, however. I call it a daily journey; others may refer to it as enlightenment.

NEW YORK CITY-OUR NEW HOME

We were issued visas to travel to New York City in May of 1975; we met our younger half-brother Leo and my sister Mari, the one who ended up giving me peace. Her love is unconditional, that I know. No matter how difficult things have been, she has always been a soft cushion for the soul. My step-mom's name was Inez. She was mom, just an amazing sight, filled with comfort, warmth, strength beauty; she eventually became the most influential woman in my life. I remember our first breakfast in the United States - two eggs sunny side up, toast and juice. This was the life. Mark and I couldn't stop laughing, we were so happy. As tears run down my face now, I am so proud of him and what he has become. I am just as proud of Leo, the philosopher and motivational speaker. These attributes were sowed by mom early on and that became her legacy and our inheritance.

(Billy is also a miracle kid, by all accounts, and I dream of bringing him to the States one day.)

OUR FIRST HOSPITAL EXPERIENCE IN THE STATES

Mark and I were way below our weight and size for our age group. Once we went to the hospital for a check-up. The doctors would made their rounds and I recall how their faces filled with pity and sadness. Their expressions will remain etched in mind. We were very ill with tapeworms, had an awful cough and were underweight. You name it, and we had it. They were in disbelief: Mark weighed about 30 lbs. and I weighed about 37. Think of the many infomercials you see about "Feed the Children." That is what we had become; Mark and I were not well. By the way, this is where we met Dr. Sandoval, the one who prescribed Robitussin, *esa baina era malicima.* To our young tongues at the time, this seemed to be the most awful cough medicine we ever had. Then, again, it wasn't like we had a pediatrician in the Dominican Republic.

Over time, it was the love of my step-mom, her compassion and relentless prayers that began to lift our spirits and improve our emotional well-being. You see, dad was never around and she assumed the role of both parents. She was the one constant who was faithful, reliable and worthy of being called a parent in my life. Please listen - dad was too busy drinking and having an affair with a woman. I will share more of this story in my next book: "Sons and Their Fathers: Why the Mess?"

HOME LIFE: THE EARLY YEARS

Those of us who grow up in an unstable and dysfunctional home environment end up with countless scars. The ones who stand out the most for me came from the malnutrition and emotional duress such as the inability to sleep and constant nightmares. These are the type of wounds that take time to heal. I found a healer in Inez. It didn't matter what the time I woke up in the middle of the night, she was there.

Now, I am not sure what you have gone through, but you have to find or allow in that one person who is trying to console your heart. You can't do this alone anymore. I know I couldn't. One thing is for sure - your stability can and will define how you rest and evolve physically, emotionally and spiritually.

SCHOOL - THE EARLY YEARS: A FATHER'S LESSON

Do you recall your favorite teacher and her name? What was it that she did to make the memory so dear to you? My 5th grade experience set the tone for my new life in the States as I faced crossroads and became eager to strive for excellence as a student. I was in Ms. Maltz's class learning my lines for the play "Grease" that had just come out as a film in the local theatres with John Travolta and Olivia-Newton John, when I was told to report for a conference with the teacher giving out test scores. She informed me that, unfortunately, I had not met the criteria for promotion and that there was a possibility that I would not be going to the 6th grade. I had achieved a below grade level 2.8 reading scale on the state assessment test.

I was devastated, folks. The one thing my dad was 'dead serious' about was school, and he had threatened Mark and me that if we ever came home with poor grades he would relinquish our immigration status and ship us back to the Dominican Republic. (By the way, the teacher also noted that I was a bit talkative in class.) Well, that afternoon my dad got home, heard my news, and began to make arrangements to send us back. This could not be happening!

Meanwhile, he had an immediate Dominican punishment for me. He went to the kitchen, got the twine and tied me up in a chair in front of an old black and white TV set without reception. He left me there for about four hours. *"Estoy halto de tus estupideses,"* he shouted, "I'm tired of your stupidity."

This became only one of my many clashes with dad. I began to experience anxiety, which eventually led to gastritis. Remember, I'm still ten years old. A few months later he invited guests over to the house and sent me on an errand to pick up a pack of Heineken beer. Back in those days, the grocery stores had a verbal agreement with parents about kids picking up the delivery. He gave me a $20 bill. I got back in five minutes with that beer; it was important to please him. He would give me a hug from time to time when he was in a good mood. Suffice it to say, however, that this time, in my haste to please, the beer was hot because I grabbed it from the shelf, not the cooler, and I left the change from the $20 in the grocery store. He made me open a bottle and drink it in one shot in the presence of his guests.

Later that night, he came in the room and got the vacuum cleaning chord and struck me enough times that I was cut and bleeding. Mom was in tears and I was just a skeletal figure getting a beating for something I should have never been asked to do as a kid.

Still, despite the physical and psychological abuse, I valued my home stability at this time. At least we were eating and not homeless, and I had Inez on my side.

A SON'S PROMISE

Years later, by the time I reached the 10th grade, school had become a real bore. I really had little interest in completing my high school diploma. I had visions of grandeur, though, and some included my dad while he called me a dreamer without action.

I recall a day mom went to school to check up on me and found that I had not been in school for about forty days. Listen very closely; this is the moment when my life truly turned around. Mom cooked the best meal ever for me when I got home that afternoon and she asked, "How was school Victor?" I couldn't lie. She knew that. All I could say was, "It was OK." Mom pulled me over to the kitchen table and I just couldn't face her. She wanted answers, reasons for these absences. I knew I had broken her heart. I couldn't live with myself. Here she was, in front of me, having cooked the best meal ever, and asking about school. She was that special. *Mi hijo, y come tu me vas hacer eso? El estudio es el arma y la luz del a*lma. I just couldn't eat that meal, I hugged her and kept a firm embraced until I promised that this would never happen again. I promised that I would go to school and change humanity. I have no idea why I would make that promise so early on but my promise meant something special to her. I just had to fulfill it. Whatever promises you have made to your loved one, you have to make them happen, no matter what. I went back to high school and graduated and mom was there. The man I called dad was not.

My advice to you is to work hard, pray, and hope that God will reveal Himself to you through scripture along the way. I went on to receive an Associate's Degree in Liberal Arts, a Bachelor's in education, Masters in Bilingual Special Education and Masters in Instructional Leadership and Supervision over 15 years ago. Mom and I always had a special celebration by ourselves.

I eventually graduated from seminary with a Doctorate in Religious Education and feel proud of this accomplishment and mom would have been proud as well, if she had lived to see it. But, why was I so empty? What was missing? Why was I still not fulfilled?

Mind you, I was able to give mom a final gift. When I was informed by the doctors that she had terminal cancer, I traveled to New York one more time and told her that I had finally been promoted to the role of Principal of a high school. Folks, it does not get better than this. You should have seen her face light up. She was so proud. I told her the doctoral studies had to be placed on hold at that time, and her response was: *"Te recuerda de la promesa?"* "Do you recall your promise, Victor?" "Make it happen" was her way of giving me wings, of being a beacon of strength, and for that I will be eternally grateful.

Yes, the blessings have been from above. For the Lord has guided, protected and molded me for this moment in my life. My children are older now and I can do so much more under His grace.

The rest of this story will be told in another book, for another day. Just remember to be blessed and know that the Lord will never forsake you. Trust me, I know. I dropped out of school at sixteen, had a daughter at twenty-one and earned a doctorate at forty-four!

The road to recovery begins when you acknowledge the strength and source of the one that laid His life on the cross that you may have eternal life.

Chapter 3:

Motivation: A Bridge to Peace

- What fuels it?
- How do you claim it?
- Where does it come from?
- Are you listening to it?

Whether it was trying to get to the States with my dad or trying to prove to him that I was not a failure in school, I had something worth fighting for. I also had help along the way, I was not alone, although there were days I thought I was in the desert. Seriously, you can't teach motivation; it's an emotion fueled with a blinding beacon of hope and righteousness. It is so much more than the need to be in a place of certainty or an elevated state of mind filled with freedom and clarity.

As I pointed out in the previous chapter, I made a promise to my mom, and honored it. She motivated me. That promise also served to motivate my future. My dad would often take me to work with him on Sunday mornings. He was a porter at high rise building. I recall one particular Sunday after my dad had been drinking the prior evening and had a terrible hangover when he really needed my help. He received a call from one of the tenants on the 15th floor to say she had a leak in the kitchen sink and there was no handyman on duty that day.

Upon entering the apartment, I couldn't help but notice the decorations and the lavish lifestyle this older lady had. It was an amazing sight: paintings, chandelier, expensive vases, white leather sectionals and rugs. This was the kind of stuff you saw in movies. Well, dad went to work in the kitchen and I remained in the living room looking around. Folks, I was so mesmerized that I knocked over a Chinese vase and it crashed onto the parquet floor. I knew I was going to get one of my dad's Dominican discipline sessions. Listen, I wanted to beat myself. I felt horrible, obligated, scared and had no idea of how to help my dad. I remember the woman's piercing and demeaning stare at my dad and his walk of shame to the kitchen to get a broom to pick up my mess. She told my dad that it was an expensive vase and he needed to pay her back for it and my dad assumed full responsibility.

We finished the cleanup and the repair and as we walked out of the apartment I remember her giving me fifty cents for helping out. I gave it right back. *Que se pensaba?Tu sabes la verguensa que yo pase?* What did she think? You know how embarrassing that was? I told her to consider it a down payment on restitution for the damages. She smiled with satisfaction and my dad and I headed to the locker room. My dad was in tears. I never saw him like that - so vulnerable, weak and helpless. His hangover was over; his face was pale as tears overwhelmed him. He was in shock and ashamed. I began to cry, too. This stuff was contagious. I wanted no part of it. I told myself that day, "Victor, you are no victim." I knew then that I would never go through such a humiliating experience again in my life. I was going to equip myself with skills; I had no idea what, but something. There was nothing I could do that day but promise that one day I would help him. My dad said that my ticket out of humiliation was an education. I promised him, then, that I would make him proud and he smiled. My dad rarely smiled. He became an orphan at four years of age and barely finished high school when he enlisted in the Navy. Much of what my dad modeled was not ideal. Drinking and listening to the most depressing "please shoot me" music was the norm from Thursday until Sunday. Raphael de Espana, Julio Iglesias, Leonardo Favio, these are a few of the great artist of his time. This was completely depressing. The fact that he smiled meant that there was still a sign that there was hope in our relationship and this is why I hold this moment as endearing. In retrospect, this is one of many incidents that drove me to excel.

AWAKENED POTENTIAL

In the last chapter I spoke about the traumatic period when my promotion to 6th grade was in doubt. Well, I was promoted, and I never stopped reading after that. Sometimes my eyes would scroll the text; other times I had to use my index finger to keep up with the storyline. I focused on reading comprehension and vocabulary. These were the two strategies Ms. Maltz told me were the secret to reading. In the Spring of that school year student conferences were held and the results of the state exams were distributed. I was the last one to come up to meet with the teacher. Listen, I was beyond gastritis - I went to the restroom three times before she got to my name on the list. When I approached her, she was in tears. Of course by now I'm thinking the worse had happened.

Instead, she told me, "Victor read this number." I replied, "8.8." "You have achieved the greatest student performance score for the entire school," she said, beaming. "You went from a 2.8 reading scale to an 8th grade reading level. We are so proud of you!" Wow, for the first time in a long time, someone had used the word proud in my presence. I was overjoyed and gained a new sense of confidence. I was transferred to the gifted class (A+ kids) for the rest of the year.

THE DESIRE TO MAKE A DIFFERENCE

Growing up on the Lower East Side of New York City in the mid-1980s was interesting. I was in search of myself and talents and I joined a number of organizations including the Environmental Action Coalition. We were assigned to work for the Parks Department cleaning parks all around the city. This was my first official job and motivation in itself, you see, because most of the kids I went to school with were busy on the corner selling drugs. I was too scared to do that and, besides, how could I possibly break my mother's heart again?

During my last year as a senior, I won a paid internship with British Petroleum in the Public Relations Department. You should have seen me: tie, jacket and slacks. This was one of the most profound experiences I ever had. I went to eat with the senior staff - the cheapest meal was $50. *Oye, dique comiendo con los ricos despues de ver pasado tanta hambre.* I later joined another youth leadership group which led to another paid stipend.

The new group I joined was a collective project with all the local high school student leaders in their schools who wanted to contribute in their community. We went to the Bowery House soup kitchen on 3rd Ave located in lower Manhattan at the time and helped feed the homeless. Afterward, we went to the church service and heard a number of men speak about their experiences as former bankers, lawyers, and doctors. I was amazed to see how many people had lost all because of drugs and they also talked about their disobedience to God. This had a significant impact on me. I don't know how often you come across a homeless person in South Florida but I can tell you, that's someone's sibling, parent, child or mate. What happened to them and how are they being helped in your community? Perhaps this is something you may want to explore. Helping others to heal and help themselves has been a crucial aspect of my life. By the way, this is about the same time I had my second awakening to Jesus.

A GLIMPSE AT A BRIDGE

I encourage you to find that one thing that moves you to act, help. Then go forward, and prepare to take the challenge. There are many mentors who are just waiting for you to act. They have been placed in your life so that you may be equipped to fulfill your unique mission.

Do you recall the movie "The Pursuit of Happiness" with Will Smith? Trust me, it happens. Life will turn around and flip things out in a second. The question is, how do you bounce back and how prepared and willing will you be to be obedient?

Sometimes things have to go wrong so that you can wake up and make sense of life. Not everything that goes wrong is bad, though. Think about it. If I had not been motivated to read, would I have had such gains in school? Would I have had the drive to win an internship where there were 200 other students in line for the spot to work for British Petroleum?

My failures in the past are but memories of hardships that have led me to this unique time and space of contentment in my life today. I turned a letter of rejection from Syracuse University into a challenge, and got into Utica College of Syracuse University. My desire to help others has always been greater than the desire to help myself so failure to get into a college was not an option. I knew I needed to leave the Lower East Side of NYC. So, stop and listen. Don't run anymore. Take a deep breath and think about the one thing that fulfills you and brings joy into your life.

Overcoming trauma, finding stability and acting on motivation are fundamental themes in our lives. Reflection on the deeply rooted memories of past experiences - even the painful ones - can help you heal. Stop and think for a moment about the promises you have made and not honored, and the need to forgive yourself for not only hurting those who dearly love you, but you as well.

You probably have many questions and would like to get some answers about how to get yourself back on the road to recovery and fulfilling your purpose. Answers to many of my questions began to appear for me about six years ago after I went in search of spiritual clarity.

I'm not suggesting that you run out and purchase a Bible, go to church every day and think that somehow this will turn things around for you magically. Not at all! Your walk with a *Divine Presence* is unique and can only commence the moment you acknowledge the need for obedience.

Chapter 4:

Gaining Clarity in Your Spiritual Life

- Have you ever truly looked into the most influential book ever written?
- Is the Bible as much an instrument of power as people claim it to be?
- Are you ready to receive a supernatural gift filled with countless treasures?

How many times have you heard someone say, "There is no perfect book that shows you what to do: just try and hope for the best"?

This is the biggest misconception. Most things are relative and subjective. One person's reality is another's perception; perception leads to judgment, judgment to conviction, and conviction leads to truth. Yet, who is in possession of the ultimate truth?

THE BIBLE AS BRIDGE

Up until now you have read about my background, early upbringing and struggles. The one thing that was always been and continues to be a constant source and beacon of hope in my life is the Word and voice of God found in Scriptures. For me it is a bridge, which I use as a simple metaphor.

What is the sole purpose of a bridge and what were the resources used in building it? A bridge connects one point to another; it is an instrument or mechanism used to get you to an intended location so that you may cross over. For instance, the famous Bay Bridge in California is the longest and most expensive in the U.S. It has undergone a major facelift since the 1989 earthquake which impacted a section. Reportedly, at least 280,000 cars cross the bridge each year.

Jesus Christ came so that we may no longer suffer. All transgressions and tribulations are dissolved by the blood and stripes on His back. Obedience gets you access to the bridge and Christ connects you to the Father through the activation of scripture. The living Christ that is within us is what gives us access to the realm of everlasting life. The Bible aligns the Father, the Son and the Holy Spirit as One so that you may partake in the presence of love, always. You see - the presence of this amazing love in the birth of a child and in the faces of parents who witness their child's first steps or when they utter their first word. Have you witnessed these events?

No other person or event in the history of mankind has had a greater spiritual impact on the blue print and fiber of our true existence. As I sit and write my thoughts on this subject, I am humbled and truly transformed. How can I possibly describe the person who has changed my life and that of future generations?

The transformation I'm referring to will only occur when you repent. Through repentance, an extraordinary and liberating catalyst takes place in the most remote part of your mind. Deep under the very crater of the darkest corner in hell, a man's soul is released into a dimension of hope, light, and everlasting companionship with the Father in the heavens. This unique spiritual transformation and experience can only materialize after you accept Jesus Christ as your Lord and Savior.

PURPOSE

The origins of the word Bible come from the Greek, meaning 'Biblia'. It is where all Holy Scriptures are stored. In essence, it is "The Holy Book" for Christians, also known as the Word of God. It contains scriptures written by men and inspired by the Holy Spirit.

The Bible is the perfect companion and guide for spiritual renewal. It contains over sixty-six books. It speaks volumes to those who want to know proverbs, poetry and historical accounts, laws, prophecy and so much more. Whether you begin with the Old Testament or open any verse or chapter, there is a remarkable transformation that takes place in the supernatural. The Bible is the mind of God; it begins with creation and ends with Revelation. It proclaims Christ as the giver of everlasting life and the only way to the Father in heaven. Without Christ's presence in your life, there is no bridge to heaven and as such there is no connection to the Father.

REVELATION OF SCRIPTURE

There are those who believe that the Bible is difficult to read. However, difficulty is a matter of attitude and conviction. Similarly, there are those who are also convinced that the Bible is too wordy and profound. Others suggest that it is deceiving. People have unstable lifestyles and allow Satan's blindfold to claim victory in their lives. Over time, ritual behaviors lead to rebellion and refusal of submission and obedience. For such an audience, there is instability, confusion, and darkness.

On the other hand, the Bible may in fact be one of the most influential, motivational and inspiring books ever written. The Bible's author is God Himself. It is written in simple, methodical and historical context. The key to understanding the Bible is accepting and complying to the instructions provided. The Bible is liberating and acts as the only source of strength to those who believe in it through acts of faith.

In the Bible, the will of God is manifested and readers receive repeated dosages of spiritual instructions. These can be found in Romans, Psalms, 2 Timothy, 2 Peter, Hebrews, Matthew, and Jeremiah. Reading, discerning and allowing the Word to be revealed evolves over time with greater clarity, worship and praise. By reading the Bible, the reader is redeemed, blessed and encouraged to persevere despite the circumstances. In addition, the act of fasting and having a personal dialogue with Christ are, perhaps, just as important.

The Bible is the book of salvation for those who believe in its content. In the event you are going through sorrow, read John 14. I did after my mother's passing. Trust me - something amazing happened because I was ready to receive the message.

Is the reader going through a fearful experience? Read Psalms 91. It is a book of spiritual guidance; it is not logical. The sacred scriptures are inspired by the thoughts of God so that mankind may find the fruits of the spirit.

Chapter 5:

Living the Word

- When do you apply what you have read?
- When do you read, and is it a part of your way of life?
- Are you reflecting at the end of the day and how did you respond to tribulations today?
- Where did you find strength and comfort?

The Kingdom of Heaven is found in the Spirit and in the manner we accept that Divine Presence in our lives.

SECOND AWAKENING

I alluded to this awakening in the previous chapters and really need to share a few more things with you. First and foremost, raising teenagers and three at that is not easy. Well not easy if you are not allowing scripture to flow and be a part of everyday living. I got caught up with pursuing an education and working long hours; this is no excuse but it is what happened. Church and doing fellowship was a foreign thing for me until I was able to meet with my first spiritual parents (pastors). Folks, I was 40 and had so many questions. My spirit was uneasy; a burning sensation on my chest was the norm by the time I got home after work. There was something so profound moving my soul, I needed to hear the voice of God and had no idea how to reach him until I met with people who shared a similar vision of servitude.

I began to attend bible study classes and after the first year was already doing bible study sessions at home. *Imaginate, di que yo estudiando la Biblia y alabando la Palabra*? Around this same time, I was able to call my biological mom in Dominican Republic and forgive her. Now that was a three hour call and a $400 bill, but it was worth it.

I even called my dad after over four years, I forgave him as well. We prayed for hours. These were divine moments in my healing. I have never been the same. I found peace and strength in this forgiveness. I suggest you try it; it's rather refreshing. I was able to sleep throughout the night after 35 years.

During this second spiritual reawakening I found peace and answers in the triple threat (fasting, scripture and alone time with our Lord). I went through countless spiritual retreats at home alone and in church. This is how I was able to slowly heal. Listen, that doesn't mean things at home were rosy, on the contrary. I had a number of Goliaths to tackle and found my guidance in scripture. This was especially the case when dealing with situations at home with the kids. I refer to these years as the exit stage years. They were finishing high school and felt they did not need a curfew or to be told what to do. Can you imagine? Well, no worries. Through the Word, I was able to remain calm, cool and collected. Seriously, I made it very clear through modeling that they were no longer my God. I stopped running to them when they got into trouble. I was there to give them advice and love them but they had been raised to be righteous, to care and leave a legacy to humanity. I love my children and have no regrets. Remember, every parent wants what's best for their children but once they got a little older everyone went their separate ways at home. We didn't have dinner together anymore or they were just too busy with friends and I continued to dive more into the Word and attend Sunday service and assist in leading our Men's ministry.

The truth is, looking back, my children were - and are - the greatest gift God has ever given me. Their teenage years were typical. The question is what was my relationship with God at that time and how did I manage? My son stopped attending school during the 10th grade year, yes, MY SON CUT SCHOOL. And, I'm a teacher. What is going on? My oldest decided to run away one weekend after her junior year (horrible day). We had a missing person's report, pictures all over the neighborhood…I can go on and on. The youngest - well, let's just say she has been in search of peace. All three of them are unique and special. Through all of this, during my stay at the church I was attending for about four years, the kids attended a few services. In fact, my oldest served in the youth ministry and the youngest received Christ as her Lord and savior. My son graduated this past year and received a BS in business and music production from Florida Atlantic University and became a dad. My girls are still in school, in search of wisdom they tell me. I know, just what every dad wants to hear, right? Either way, I must have read Proverbs 3:1-12 (NIV) at least a hundred times:

"My son, do not forget my teaching, but keep my commands in your heart, for they will prolong your life many years and bring you peace and prosperity….."

Listen, it has not been peachy, but we are family and we love each other NO MATTER WHAT. During the last two years, I kind of lost of myself in the shovel of life but I made it back to the Kingdom recently and I will never be the same. I have recommitted my life to serving Christ. Yes it's that simple. I repent, and hold on to trust and hope that I will be humble and worthy of receiving His favor.

It is within the context of this second awakening that I found the tools to return to a place of sanctity. This is one of the reasons why I am inspired to write in the Spirit about the Apostle Paul. The irony behind the man that persecuted Christ is remarkable; I suppose theologians continue to draw conclusions about Paul's role in the church and do so simply because of the current challenges faced by humankind.

Paul was by all account truly brilliant. Through the scriptures, he is able to rescue us from darkness and lead us into the light. Obedience to the law, forgiveness and love of humanity are all behaviors that are driven by grace and Divine Presence. Most people take a lifetime to reflect on this statement and that's all right. I will humbly argue that it's a matter of timing and alignment. We are spiritual beings and are ultimately conditioned and molded by our emotions and thoughts, convictions and passions. The secret behind dismantling the disorder in your life is to remember how to react when confronted with the impurities and mistrust of the secular world. Paul provides a snapshot of what that means in the following verse. These are the chain links (behaviors) that bind the spirit into enslavement. Are any of these behaviors prevalent in today's society?

Galatians 5: 22-24 tells us:

"The acts of the sinful nature are obvious: sexual immorality, impurity and debauchery; idolatry and witchcraft; hatred, discord, jealousy, fits of rage, selfish ambition, dissensions, factions and envy; drunkenness, orgies, and the like. (I warn you, as I did before, that those who live like this will not inherit the kingdom of God.)

But the fruit of the Spirit is love, joy, peace, patience, kindness, goodness, faithfulness, gentleness and self-control. Against such things there is no law. Those who belong to Christ Jesus have crucified the sinful nature with its passions and desires."

I will look upon the Lord, seek that kingdom and proclaim my inheritance. This revelation has prompted me to write this book. Although the secular world may try to bind us, the fruit of the

Spirit is liberating. When one is truly liberated through the revelation of the Word and is willing to walk-the-walk in faith, all things are possible because of the covenant that is made through the act of obedience.

THE AWAKENED SPIRIT: HOW DID I GET OUT OF DARKNESS?

How did I overcome depression at an early age? What prompted me to search for answers and help others? How was I evolving in the Spirit and what led me to a place of sanctity?

The answer is not about religion, but rather a unique relationship with the Creator. My journey and walk in faith was inconsistent up until six years ago. I was not obedient. I found a new church, however, and began a spiritual renewal. I also went through a year of Biblical training and servitude with my pastors. I don't think of myself as a Pastor, although there are days that the characteristics of pastorship surround me.

I am convinced that the Presence of righteousness is indeed my best friend because it is what allows me to be aligned with the Kingdom while operating in the secular world. For me that occurred through a spiritual awakening.

Once I decided that I needed a change in my life, it became the unique moment that paved the way for an emotional and spiritual transformation. As I began reading the verses in the morning, about 4:00 a.m. - the best time - I noticed that I was no longer reading them as texts but rather as a conversation with the authors.

I was deeply moved by the message of encouragement. The texts were purifying, and constructed the necessary spiritual foundation for my lifestyle (way of life). I no longer feel surprised at events that unfold at work or in my daily life. I am comforted to be embraced by the Word of God. I realize that there are countless people out there with the same problems I have encountered.

WHAT IS IT ABOUT SCRIPTURE THAT AWAKENS US?

Bible texts from the Psalmist, James, Hebrews, Romans and Ephesians have rejuvenated and influenced how and when I get connected to the bridge of righteousness. I now understand clearly that I have the power to control my immediate environment regardless of what I'm exposed to. I am under grace and moved by faith, not by what I see around me. This is simply a decision. Is this the type of journey you want to make? Trust in God and He will show you the way.

When was the last time you attended service in church? What happened that day? How active is the Spirit of God in your life? These are crucial questions that only you can answer. You have to make the decision to make a change. Don't expect for things to change until you commit to that one thing that keeps holding you back.

There is a spiritual warfare going on in your life and the questions are: Are you ready for the change? How can you bring light into the abyss? Are you prepared to go and get your soul back? What will it take?

Light first entered my life at the age of four in the Dominican Republic as I elaborated in the earlier chapters. While in search of my biological mom one day, I found three pesos under a rock. How about that? We had a meal that day-out of nothing there was something. At sixteen, I decided to drop out and attend a trade business school. I needed a pair of pants, size 28, grey denim. I didn't have the money to purchase them. Well, I went to the store to get a soda and there were two men waiting by the cashier register-they asked me: "Can you use a pair of pants?" This was a little bizarre but I said "Sure." They gave it to me wrapped in a brown paper bag. When I got home I opened it in front of mom. Guess what? These were the same pair pants I needed. How about the day I failed my teaching boards by one point? I went to scripture Psalms 91; I don't know why. But I can tell you that the next time I took the exam I had a perfect score. I say, to God be the glory always. These events were isolated and yet filled with light. I found the light during the worst of times, in moments of despair and helplessness. The Lord's presence continued to manifest itself in my life. Folks, it stopped being logical for me. My understanding of faith was becoming real, a natural part of living. The thing is it wasn't always consistent.

I am not here to tell you that you can do this overnight; it takes divine time and obedience. Paul States it well; self-control will be a fundamental behavior that needs to be tamed. How will this transformation occur in you? In the next two sections we will conduct a close study of Scripture and let it become the guide.

PART TWO

A LAMP TO LIGHT THE WAY

Chapter 6:

Light Charges and Transforms

- Where does light resonate from and end?
- Once darkness enters, can you summon the light so that you may find the truth?
- Is light uncompromised?
- What purpose does it serve you today?

People, struggle is part of life. I have found that there is way out of the struggle, though - through prayer, worship and busy work. Yes, keep busy, keep writing, and keep helping. You will come out of it. I did, and this is how:

Step I: Listen to the lyrics found in Hezekiah Walker's "Every Praise", Lighthouse's "Everything" and Josh Groban's "Don't Give Up":

Step II: Reflect on the mystery scripture for the day. There is a remarkable and supernatural event that occurs when we attend service or just worship on our own. Look at David's Psalms 18: "The Lord is your fortitude and comfort. You are redeemed, saved and anointed to do great works." (NIV)

By creating a daily reading and writing plan you invite a thing called wisdom into your life (see Proverb 3-NIV). The growth process will then create a springboard for the expression of your soul's desire to yell out for hope. It is here where you must let God be God. This is where the fuel is generated-write a daily plan, search and find one that accommodates you and only you. I suggest you start with Psalms, at least in the beginning. Start getting into prayer groups or talk to family members. Again, this is about how you interact with the word. It is a spiritual growth plan, a retreat for you to reconnect.

SCRIPTURE REVEALED

I was privileged to conduct my first sermon in church several years ago. I will share it with you later because it's part of the healing process that needs to take place in your life in order for you to move forward. These two steps are a springboard for what's to be revealed to you. The purpose of light is to awaken the soul, to bring life into the most remote parts of your inner being and in the Bible you will find yourself again. It's through the love light of Christ Jesus that you will enter a place called Eden again that you may be all for the Kingdom of heaven.

Key Verses: Isaiah 58:8, 42:16, Psalms 18:28, 36:9, 43:3, 119:105, Colossians 1:16-17, John 8:12, Genesis 14-17, John 8:12, Job 38: 19, 20, 24 (NIV)

Did you know that there are about 235 verses related to light in the Bible? Most can be found in Job 31 (13%), Psalms 24 (10%) and Isaiah 22 (10%).

Have you ever considered being without it? How does light impact our everyday routine and standard of living? Communications, transportation, mobility, human interactions and the need to survive may very well depend on the quickness and efficacy of that energy or electrical power being delivered to its intended source which is you, brothers and sisters.

These scriptures demonstrate how light repairs, compensates and delivers us all from the influence of the Defeated One. In the absence of light, what can the lonely see and expect?

Why is it that so often we see this misery in the eyes of the forgotten ones - the children who, without recourse, are left by the wayside without hope. I know. I was one of them. I was alone for a very long time. The physical loneliness rips your soul from grace. How? By living each day without sanctuary you are consumed with everyday ritualistic endeavors.

It is within this context that Christ can break through and bring you into peace when you accept Him. You may be facing a very difficult choice and need a sense of direction. Ask Christ to give you a hand and he will lift you out of misery as he did for me. I will elaborate further as you read along but for now look at Psalms 36: "For with you is the fountain of life; in your light we see light." (NIV)

It has often been said that individuals have clouded thoughts and these have made them act viciously and callously. I ask you, is this of Christ our Lord? Is this the type of behavior he warned us about?

These emotions are cruel and intended for a purpose - to divide, conquer and kill. Rather, consider this brother and sisters: love is, above all things, the greatest gift given to man so that he may partake in distributing it to all who embrace it.

How would light rekindle the heart and bring birth to hope and vanquish the roots of darkness? In Psalms 18:28 we get some answers. Call on the Lord and he will provide guidance: "You, O LORD, keep my lamp burning; my God turns my darkness into light."

Are you a lighthouse, a beacon of hope? Will you turn it around and allow for Christ to deliver the light of everlasting life to others? Is your lighthouse filled with the necessary energy given to you by the grace of God to do His purpose? Though strong winds may come to interrupt you and your loved ones, consider the Source that is in you through Christ Jesus that you may not be discouraged to fight the good fight.

I am amazed to discover that we are all commanded by God to behave according to the purpose for which we were created. Yes, this includes the moon, sun and the stars. But here is where it gets interesting folks. Let's look at Genesis 14-17: (NIV)

"God said, 'Let there be lights in the expanse of the sky to separate the day from the night, and let them serve as signs to mark seasons and days and years, and let them be lights in the expanse of the sky to give light on the earth." Does this mean I will experience moments of great fortune and at times, great sadness? Were season deliberately designed for a purpose? Was is it to increase our faith?

Have you noticed that the more we dive into the word, the more questions are generated and your soul slowly awakens?

In verse 14 we find that light is constant, regardless of the seasons. Whatever the season you are going through today, rest and do not despair, for the presence of our Lord Jesus Christ is with you always. Imagine: the moon, stars and sun have been placed at your disposal to provide insight as to where to go.

Make the right decision today and be cleansed for the rest of your life. You have a purpose; you have been intricately designed by divine intervention from your inception.

Your vision requires light, and light can only travel as a result of your behavior and attitude. In fact, consider all that is good, pure and humble, channeled by love, targeting misery, loneliness, frustration, ambiguity and the foundation of the ground or sea you travel on.

It's just a matter of faith (I will explain that as well in subsequent chapters).

Turn the switch on and He will command it to be so. You have never been alone. How can the blind see without physical light? They see by what they feel and what they feel is fueled by light and that light was created by Him so that no one is left blind ever. The Psalmist tells us how:

Psalms 43:3 "Send forth your light and your truth, let them guide me; let them bring me to your holy mountain, to the place where you dwell."

These verses are very symbolic and speak directly to the individual who reads it as such. There is no magic, folks. This is the way the Spirit guides when you believe. The word of God is uncompromising, faithful and constant.

Chapter 7:

Faith and Light: The Balance

- Where can I find the fuel of light?
- Once acquired, what will I do with it and how will I manage?
- Is this fuel something that can be shared with others?
- Who do you know in your life that is able to bring this sense of nourishment?

The prophet Isaiah speaks to us about guidance and the Lord's promise through scripture. I realize that those who read this chapter may have other insight but I humbly submit to what it activates within me at this time. The Lord's mercy is great, loving and everlasting. It's simple; it transforms!

Isaiah 42:16 (NIV)

"I will lead the blind by ways they have not known, along unfamiliar paths I will guide them; I will turn the darkness into light before them and make the rough places smooth. These are the things I will do; I will not forsake them."

In order for you to be aligned to what is being asked through the Spirit you must not settle for conformity and allow yourself to fall into complacency?

When you allow the light of our Lord to shed meaning on what you are about to embark upon, the level of clarity and insight is blinding - so focused and so truthful. That is what I call a supernatural truth. It does not require the endorsement or validity of men. It is righteous.

I've met with people who had strong purpose and vision of what they wanted to do in life. Some of these people became my mentors. They guided me and protected my soul and gave me hope. I listened to what they had to say and they pushed me and they valued my opinions about a better tomorrow.

I often spoke about the under-dog, the one that lost hope. This was my mission - to help those in need. It was not always easy. I had to dig deep inside and find the real Victor - the homeless kid from the Dominican Republic; the one who slept on the floor and went hungry for days; the kid who went through depression and was told that he would not amount to anything in life. Trust me, this is not about feeling sorry for yourself. There is no time for that because, if you stay in that state of mind, there will be no spiritual awakening.

In essence, think of it this way: the devil cannot hear your thoughts. He can only hear what you allow him to because of what is revealed through your speech, the tone in which you say it and how your heart is moved by that emotion at that time.

IDENTITY IS REFINED

Who are you if not the total sum of your father's generations? Who other than your father claims to have a right over you and what you represent? What is the DNA that supports this claim over time? When Jesus was brought again to defend himself against the Pharisees, He announced his name and the Father's identity but they were not willing to listen. Why is humanity stubborn? What supernatural act must occur before we are aligned on the bridge of sanctity?

In John 8:12 (NIV) we find the validity of faith through the light of Christ. It is here that the heavens open and magnify who He is in concert with such light that it may indeed bring us all closer to redemption, sanctification and the required acknowledgement of obedience and free will. When Jesus spoke again to the people, he said, "I am the light of the world. Whoever follows me will never walk in darkness, but will have the light of life."

Will this light of life be in your jobs or career? Will it be in your marriage and the relationship with your children? Will it reflect on your purpose?

How that light is rejuvenated, transformed and kindled for an eternity can only be determined by acknowledging our identity through Christ Jesus and the consistency that prevails through the stewardship of the Holy Spirit.

RELATIONSHIPS AND THE ACTS OF FAITH

Why is Jesus the great connector and how does your relationships with Him bring light to the forgotten ones? Who in your family manages to keep everyone together? Who is the life of the party? Who do you turn to in your hour of need? Why is it that this person has all the answers? Why do you confide in these people and what kind of love and peace resonate from their presence? They are guided by something uniquely granted to them – talents that are like a divine genetic trait.

GUIDING PRINCIPLES OF UNITY & RIGHTEOUSNESS

I can identify several elements that describe the holding of a substance or of a people together over time. Think of the bridge, what holds it together and allows movement from one end to the other. I trust in Christ because He knew me in my mother's womb, Christ holds all things together in light. He is the center of it all. Let us discuss Colossians 1:22-23 (NIV):

"Once you were alienated from God and were enemies in your minds because of your evil behavior. But now he has reconciled you by Christ's physical body through death to present you holy in his sight, without blemish and free from accusation—if you continue in your faith, established and firm, not moved from the hope held out in the gospel."

In conclusion, consider the importance of light, that which was ordered by God to give you clarity.

Where does light reside and darkness begin? The way for that passage has been defined by Jesus Christ's zeal on the cross and the redemption that comes through the blood that was spilled on that Holy mount.

Light is wisdom everlasting. It shelters and provides smooth landing fields in the midst of chaos. Paul conveys a poignant declaration on faith and obedience in Romans 1-5. Consider verse 5: "Through him and for his name's sake, we received grace and apostleship to call people from among all the Gentiles to the obedience that comes from faith."

Chapter 8:

The Essence of Righteousness

- What is justice and is it divine?
- Where in the law is the voice of God?
- Have you ever found yourself in its path and what did you feel?
- Have you ever been filled with and in awe of God's favor and the scent of Christ?

As I look back at my experiences, the seeds of righteousness had been planted in me when I first accepted Christ in that church re-enactment of the crucifixion over 30 years ago. I pray that in my firm decisions I may remember the act of perseverance as it is written in James 1:12 (NIV):

"Blessed is the man who perseveres under trial, because when he has stood the test, he will receive the crown of life that God has promised to those who love him."

Staying firm and focused in my decision, according to the will of God, will enable me to do his work. Ephesians 2:10 (NIV) says, "For we are God's workmanship, created in Christ Jesus to do good works, which God prepared in advance for us to do."

What does staying firm in my decision on this journey mean? It means I must deny the influence of desires so that these do not blemish my conviction in Christ. My prayer for you is that you may receive guidance from the Holy Spirit and that you may be filled with goodness and self-control. I was looking through a couple of passages in 2 Peter 3 and found a wealth of advice in (V) 5-8:

2 Peter 1:5-8 "For this very reason, make every effort to add to your faith goodness; and to goodness, knowledge; and to knowledge, self-control; and to self-control, perseverance; and to perseverance, godliness; and to godliness, brotherly kindness; and to brotherly kindness, love."

Impulsive behaviors are a result of your need to get immediate satisfaction. How and when this occurs can be traced back to your initial thoughts. Your mind has a tremendous amount of power in influencing your emotions. Your emotions are guided by the heart. What the heart desires is, by all accounts, peace.

Listen, I was young just like you. I, too, became madly in love with a childhood sweetheart and moved in with her after she got pregnant. The problem was that I was not ready to be a dad at a young age without an education or skill. Life was difficult but I grew up rather quickly after my daughter was born and I moved on with my life. (Yes, I broke it off eventually but it cost me so much. I lost myself.) Of course, love knocked on the door again and I married. Perhaps, this needs further discussion; I mean I lived that life for 22 years. I held three jobs and went on to college. Please don't think my life was as peachy as it may be portrayed today. Today I'm blessed by the Lord's mercy on my life. Today's behavior is dictated by faith and not emotion. I wake up praising and stay praising all day because it is the safest place for me. I am in awe of God's continued presence in my life and will never again have it any other way.

HOW I ARRIVED AT THIS CONCLUSION

Ann J. Polya, (a researcher on emotional intelligence) found that there are five strategies you can employ in an effort to control your emotions to get to or stay in that peace. Let me highlight these and place it the context of my experiences and how I managed my actions from a logical perspective.

1) Avoid repeated exposure to the situation. "…we need to reduce our exposure to the thing or person who spurs this emotion… (p. 90)". For instance, stop listening to the song if it reminds you of the problem, situation or people that have the same issues. Listen, you know exactly what I am referring to, especially after you break up with the one person you thought was the ONE.

2) Another approach is to: "Modify the circumstances: …find alternative activities (p.91)". Instead of reliving the dreadful experience, get started on a project you have been trying to complete but never had the time. Go and find "you." What is it that you have dying to do and never had a chance to do it because someone was holding you back? Go play an instrument, start writing, take dancing or cooking lessons or photography. I am so serious; you will heal. I promise you, you will be lifted and filled with an insurmountable amount of strength.

3) Think about switching the focus: "Consider what provoked the feeling (p.91)". Become aware of your calling in life and what moves you to act and help others or just serve. When you find your purpose and calling in life, you shift the negative thoughts into positive ones and in return you are now in control of the environment. Smile, smile, because it's about to happen; you are about to move mountains.

4) You may want to "Reappraise and Reinterpret... This can be a powerful deterrent to depression, panics and phobias (p.92)".

5) [Respond proactively to disappointments]: "Move forward; we can consider alternate plans of action and then we adopt one to move forward and put it into place (p.93)."

Instead of reflecting on what has been lost, change the dynamics of the incident and turn it to your advantage. Turn it around. In fact, writing this book has been instrumental in my healing process. This is why I continue to encourage you, brothers and sisters.

Surrounding yourself with people that share the same vision and mission may be a good start. Joining a church revival may be another. Just go out and make it happen because it will not happen if you stay home feeling sorry for yourself.

Chapter 9:

How to Become an Effective Spiritual Leader

- Who is the perfect spiritual role model and why?
- Have you identified a biblical figure that has had an impact on the effects and causality of mind over body?
- Have you gone into the deep and discovered the essence of hidden treasures found in daily scripture?

Think about your own experiences and how you apply the principles behind the parables in Mathew 20:1-16 (NIV).

This is one of those verses that makes one wonder how unique and keen our Lord Jesus was in His instructions to the disciples. What was the message? How did it impact each of them and how were they able to apply these instructions in the future? How did these fuel and arm the human spirit?

I am reminded of how I was able to move from one position to another in the teaching profession. It is an intense and often competitive career field. Many instructors believe that they have a legitimate right to remain fixed on the content or ritual delivery that is currently viewed as antiquated.

When I first entered the teaching field twenty years ago, teachers in a department viewed a person who moved up the ranks from teacher assistant to administrator with envy, dislike, and rumors were often the end result. I wondered about this, though: I went to college, earned degrees and certifications, studied, applied an ethical work standard of excellence and was willing to be humbled throughout my journey in the craft. Was this the key? Had they not experienced the same journey? Why did they have so much resentment?

As I look at verses 1-16, Jesus is very clear about timing and the carefully orchestrated alignment of grace. For instance, He sent the disciples on a quarter cycle - that is every three hours the labor recruiter found those in need - and they accepted the job and became obedient.

Once you have received your marching orders to serve, do not remain still. You are equipped by grace to complete the task. Do not fear, do not boast, for the Lord is watching.

"...'Why have you been standing here all day long doing nothing?'" 'Because no one has hired us,' they answered. "He said to them, 'You also go and work in my vineyard.'"

As a member of the Kingdom, one receives the benefits of eternal life once you have accepted Christ

Jesus. There is no room for ambiguity; therefore, regardless of when you enter, it does not matter. You will be blessed according to the fruits of your labor, for if indeed, you gained wisdom at the end, you're entitled to be just as much an inheritor as the first. Indeed, look at Romans 6:22-23 (NIV):

"When you were slaves to sin, you were free from the control of righteousness. What benefit did you reap at that time from the things you are now ashamed of? Those things result in death! But now that you have been set free from sin and have become slaves to God, the benefit you reap leads to holiness, and the result is eternal life. For the wages of sin is death, but the gift of God is eternal life in Christ Jesus our Lord."

Again, look at the second prisoner on the cross. He was guaranteed a seat in heaven because of faith.

Luke 23:41-43 (NIV):

"But the other criminal rebuked him. 'Don't you fear God,' he said, 'since you are under the same sentence? We are punished justly, for we are getting what our deeds deserve. But this man has done nothing wrong.' Then he said, 'Jesus, remember me when you come into your kingdom.' Jesus answered him, 'I tell you the truth, today you will be with me in paradise'."

I think that the responsibility of the leader is to seek the Kingdom at all times. However, for me it implies waking up in the morning and remaining faithful to the word and applying what we have read for that specific day or event. Like the farmer who needs assistance, we need to go forth and spread the Gospel and seek those in need of "work" so that they may enter the Kingdom.

Chapter 10:

My First Sermon

- Do you know you come from royalty?
- Are you aware you have a great commission?
- Did you see yourself in the mirror today and what did you really see?
- Do you know where you're from?

After a year of being in church and in training, I had an opportunity to do my first sermon. It was exciting because for the first time I was going to deliver a message of hope to my new found friends in church. This was also about the time where I had fasted for about 40 days and prayed for greater insight into scripture. I share it now with you:

Introduction

I begin with praising His name and giving Him all the glory. I thank you Lord for bringing us together this evening so that we may exalt you and feel your Holy Presence through this message throughout the presentation. Tonight I declare in the name of Jesus that the Holy Spirit fills this place with love, understanding and revelation.

May your hearts and minds be recharged, restored and strengthened in knowing that you have a greater role in life through Christ Jesus. The Word of our Lord is promising and faithful in all tribulations.

What is Fear?

Fear is an emotional response to threats and danger.

What is an Ambassador?

An ambassador is the highest ranking diplomat who represents their country. Usually Ambassadors are assigned abroad to a political post or to an international organization, to serve as the official representative of his or her own country.

In The Image of God

John 1:1-5 (NIV) "In the beginning, there was the Word, and the Word was God. He was with God in the Beginning."

Jesus was present when the world was created. Despite our tribulations, we must not doubt who we are. In fact, we were made in his image and as such God was pleased (Genesis 1: 27, 31). Our body has intricate systems of operations. Each cell has a purpose; as it evolves and adapts to the environment, so do we. As forces of change, our spirit through Christ Jesus brings balance, peace and harmony to all that surrounds us.

THE BIRTH OF AN AMBASSADOR

The creation of an ambassador is described by the Psalmist when he says:" for you were created in my inmost being; you knit me together in my mother's womb, I praise you because I am fearfully and wonderfully made; your works are wonderful, I know that full well. (Psalms 139:13-14) NIV.

Our lord and Savior was focused on crafting us as admirable beings. This is of particular interest, specifically as we look at the creation of the ambassadorship from its inception. Unique, natural intricate skills and gifts have been granted to you so that you may complete your task. Why do you suppose you have always been ahead? Why have you always been asked to lead, to participate, to complete the task? Why are you so natural at it? I'm talking about dancing, singing, manipulating numbers, organizing, decorating, and serving. All of these have been a part of my life but none has had such an impact as the use and application of languages and teaching. Folks, those of you reading this passage, search your spirit and look deep inside the experiences and the sounds these experiences have made in your heart. Where have these gifts come from?

TRAITS OF THE OFFICE FORGED IN CHRIST JESUS

Here is what's fundamental, Christ is the bread of life and whoever accepts him will never be hungry because he lives in us. John 6: 37-39 says: "All that the Father gives me will come to me, and whoever comes to me I will never drive away. For I have come down from heaven not to do my will but to do the will of him who sent me, that I shall lose none of that he has given me, but raise them up at the last day." (NIV)

Clearly, Christ Jesus was highlighting the mandate of the Kingdom to his disciples. As such, since Christ is in me, I, too, shall do my Father's will.

Benefits of an Ambassador through the Holy Spirit

1) Were you aware that all that belongs to you comes directly from the father? In fact, the unknown becomes real as revealed through the Spirit.

John 16: 15 (NIV): "All that belongs to the Father is mine. That is why I said the Spirit will take from what is mine and make it known to you."

2) An ambassador's radar allows you to stay focused and determined in faith. Despite the attacks that superimpose our everyday life, as ambassadors we are anchored through obedience and consistency. We are committed in fidelity to be on full alert at all times.

1 Peter 5:8-9(NIV): "Be self-controlled and alert. Your enemy the devil prowls around like a roaring lion looking for someone to devour. Resist him standing firm in the faith because you know that your brothers throughout the world are undergoing the same kind of suffering." This command reasserts our strength in knowing that we can handle the fight at all times.

3) You are an Heir in faith and in divine lineage. As an ambassador, do away with old clothing in thoughts and behaviors and receive your sainthood through Christ Jesus. You were chosen by God in the same manner as many of the great writers of the Old Testament. What can be said about Moses, Elijah, Esther, Daniel and David's transformation as a result of their faith and obedience? I have referred to role models in the previous chapter, I have identified these as part of my spiritual evolution. Their writings have often redirected my spirit when I have been challenged.

Colossians 3:12 (NIV): "Therefore, as God's chosen people, holy and dearly loved, clothe ourselves with compassion, kindness, humility, gentleness and patience."

4) What is the language of the ambassador? Are they evasive, or direct? Are they crystal clear when they explain a thought or propose an agenda item? This is certainly the case with our Lord Jesus Christ. How do ambassadors react to tribulations and what is the language they use to dismantle the issues? James gives us the boundaries and platform of conduct of speech.

a) James 1:2 (NIV) says: "Consider it pure joy, my brothers, whenever you face trials of many kinds, because you know that the testing of your faith develops perseverance. Perseverance must finish its work so that you may be mature and complete, not lacking anything."

How often have you been tempted and tried? Have you passed the test? Are you going through it today?

b) Tame the tongue: Ambassadors make their point without having to fight a war. The tongue is sweet but it can also be swift and wicked.

James 3: 9-11 (NIV): "With the tongue we praise our Lord and Father, and with it we curse men, who have been made in God's likeness. Out of the same mouth come praise and cursing. Can both fresh water and salt water flow from the same spring?"

CONCLUSION

The role of the ambassador is a unique one because it is the essential means by which we reconnect with Christ our Lord and Savior. The way we behave and articulate our thoughts will define our consistency in faith through the Holy Spirit.

We are rejuvenated, purified, edified, and re-clothed each day as we live by the Spirit of Christ. Therefore, we have been crafted to preach the word as inheritors with a birthright. We are driven and nurtured by the fruit of the Spirit.

We dismantle lies and promote the truth in Christ Jesus through Paul's writings in Galatians. This is the truth. All else is superficial, designed to separate you from righteousness and the apostolic appointment that is found in the Gospels. Remember, the Grace of God will be your shadow and where your spirit wills to dwell.

Chapter 11:

Salvation

- What is salvation and how can you achieve it?
- Is salvation a quest?
- Are your prepared to give everything up in life to achieve it?
- What must I do to preserve my salvation and what role will obedience play?

NATURE OF JESUS

In asking who is Jesus Christ, the answers may vary depending on the person's spiritual background, affiliations, church dynamics and/or regions of the world - particularly in Asia, Africa, South and Central America and the U.S. . The deeply rooted belief that Christ died for our sins is a primordial and focal point of the Christian Church.

Consider the terrorist attacks of September 11, 2001 on the World Trade Towers, and the Pentagon, the thousands of lives that were lost and its lingering aftermath for those of us that remained in everlasting prayer. It was Christ Jesus that calmed the storm. No other figure in the face of history would have been able to assemble so many on the steps of a global spiritual community. For many, this was a tragic event. Others, however, consider it one of the holiest of days, as God himself could be felt through the grace of His only begotten Son who brought peace and calmness into the hearts of the afflicted.

Christ is embedded in the mosaic of the millennia. Consider, if you will, the many celebrations that take place throughout the year. For instance, Easter, and Christmas have been commercialized, yet, at the very core of the celebration is the belief that Christ died on the cross for the sins of humanity so that whoever believes may inherit the Kingdom of heaven.

THE NATURE OF SALVATION

"The word "salvation" occurs the following number of times in the following translations of the Bible: English Standard Version (166), American Standard Bible (159), King James Version (158), New King James Version (156), New American Standard Bible(156) times, Revised Standard Version (127)and in the New International Version (118) times. Consider the following chapters in Romans: 1:16, 10:9, and chapters in Acts:4:12, 13.46-47, 16:30-34.

The same doctrine of salvation permeates other books of the New Testament. Mark's Gospel ends with this missionary charge in 16:15-17 (KJV):

"And he said unto them, Go ye into all the world, and preach the gospel to every creature. He that believeth and is baptized shall be saved; but he that believeth not shall be damned."

We live in a world of uncertainty, a world made up of principalities that look into the very core of those in need and capitalize on their weaknesses, causing divisions and separating families - which ultimately leads to spiritual death. We are the sheep and Christ Jesus is our Shepherd. We have nothing to long for when we activate our identity in Him. The love of God for humanity transcends all dimensions and even though we were sinners, Christ fulfilled the prophecies and was crucified for our transgressions.

This debt is paid in full and as brothers of Christ we are, through the Gospels, declared debt free. Our brotherhood in Christ is constant, revived and strengthened through our faith and love of God. As we are reborn through the Spirit, we are no longer driven by circumstances and events.

All things are discerned through the Spirit and it is through the Spirit that I choose to live and be obedient. I am guided and revitalized through the daily scriptures and I am able to produce good fruit in the midst of those ever-surging storms.

The moment we are saved, we embark on a remarkable transformation. Even before the birth of humanity, God had already designed the plan of salvation.

In Jeremiah, 31:3 (KJV) the author's insight is soothing and assures the reader of God's love of mankind: "The LORD hath appeared of old unto me, saying, Yea, I have loved thee with an everlasting love: therefore with loving kindness have I drawn thee."

As he majestically draws you to Him, you receive salvation and access to the Kingdom of heaven.

Because of the living Christ in you and God's love, you have the promise and assurance that all things are possible. Your attitude, obedience and conviction will ultimately bring you closer to Him.

PART THREE

ASSURANCE

Chapter 12:

The Assurance

- What does assurance mean and how does it connect us to Christ, the bridge of glory?
- Why is your debt paid in full and who is your deliverer?

I think of assurance as a seal. It's about confidence - the confidence we have in a factual event like turning your car ignition on, or getting inside an elevator and trusting that it will take you to the desired destination.

I wonder though - what if the engine does not turn on. What if the elevator rails snap and assurance is but a memory. When parts of major air conditioning and heating systems are designed, manufactured, distributed and installed around the world, don't they place a seal of inspection indicating – assuring - that a high level or standard has been met? Don't you expect the merchandise to work?

Consider if you will a different analogy - the Olympic trainee who, through time and training runs countless miles in pursuit of the ultimate gold medal. There is a high level of competition on the field. Every athlete looks good, is in great shape and is visibly aggressive. On the final lap of the course, however, something remarkable happens. In the Spirit, there is an extraordinary rush that expands through every muscle, artery and vein and the breathing complements the ultimate move. One person on the track will rise to the challenge with assurance, looking behind and ahead and, in a matter of seconds, pulling in front and conquering the field.

RECONNECTING

Close your eyes and inhale deeply. Breathe out for five seconds and repeat this sequence for about thirty seconds, and begin to praise and worship Him as you reconnect with His divine presence. There are countless praise and worship songs available, these are within your grasp.

Now open your Bible to Ephesians 2:18 and allow this verse to speak to you: "For through him we both have access by one Spirit unto the Father."

Paul's letter to the Ephesians reveals to us a spiritual bridge that ultimately opens to Eden. This kind of assurance is the salvation of Christ in our lives.

Assurance cannot be dependent on feelings, as feelings betray us. My salvation does not exist as a result of my good works. Rather, it is through affirming faith, remaining in a daily walk with Christ and applying the daily scriptures that I may find my way back to Eden. The Word of God tells us that the devil is always in search of souls - preying, watching and finally devouring without warning. How do we prepare for the battle?

The unseen fight is waged in the minds of man, on the way to work, when you get into a car accident, when you failed to meet a deadline and fear you have now jeopardized a career.

This is one of the reasons I have made the decision to stay connected. I urge you to examine the following verse very carefully - 1 John 4:13 (KJV):

"Hereby know that we dwell in him, and he in us, because he hath given us of his Spirit."

In essence, the love of our Lord resides in you, and in me. As such, I decide to be obedient and follow the righteous path and His commandments. There is no force - whether visible or invisible - that can pull a saved person from the authority and presence of our Lord Christ.

Paul's writing in Romans tells us to remain persuaded in the Word, that these forces (tribulations, sorrow, depression, anger,) are multidimensional and evident in the sight of all existence, as described in chapter 8:38-39.

Once I receive Christ as my Lord and Savior, there is nothing that can take my spirit, soul and mind from Him. Imagine: this includes the angels in heaven. No one can separate us from the love of Christ. Don't you ever forget this message - you are made in the image of God. No matter where you are, remember, you are holy.

Similarly, Romans 12:2 directs us to rebuke and dismiss conformity of what is seen in the world. What are those things that keep us in chains? Addictions, fear, lack of prosperity? These things of the world manipulate the mind, which in turn manipulates the heart and, as such, stirs the emotions. Therefore, protect your mind, with the helmet of salvation and shield of faith.

Take, for instance, an obsession with shopping on-line, or watching television or simply listening to music. What do all these things have in common? When you place your spirit and soul in the midst of carnal desires, you have just become a target for the evil one to take control of your thoughts. This is where he operates and dictates your mood and passion. Just remember, what have you committed yourself to? How will this behavior edify the body of Christ? Have you made a covenant with the cross and, if so, how will you lead others to the footsteps of heaven?

In summary, Ephesians 6:16-18 gives us further assurance so that we may remain under the cover of protection:

"Above all, taking the shield of faith, wherewith ye shall be able to quench all the fiery darts of the wicked. And take the helmet of salvation, and the sword of the Spirit, which is the word of God: Praying always with all prayer and supplication in the Spirit, and watching thereunto with all perseverance and supplication for all saints...."

These darts that Paul speaks about come from all directions. We need to be reminded of how to discern and prepare to respond to life in grace and how to remain covered in the great glory of Christ Jesus. Fanny Crosby had it right when she wrote: "Blessed assurance, Jesus is mine; Oh what a foretaste of glory divine. Heir of salvation, purchase of God; Born of His Spirit, washed in His blood."

My advice is a simple yet very difficult one to put into action without faith. Walking alone without the guidance and comfort of a spiritual leader (pastor or priest) can be exhausting and it doesn't have to be that way. Trust me, I lived that life for over 35 years and will tell you it drained me. Don't you dare go it at alone anymore, it just doesn't work. It doesn't.

Things began to change in me after I was baptized, as I indicated in the prior chapters. My second awakening paved the way and provided the foundation for me to remain connected and find the tools necessary to come back to light, despite problems at home and work. I faced countless challenges in my career and found wisdom in Proverbs when dealing with my teenaged children turned 17, 18, and 19 years old. You may be currently going through it now. If so, stop and listen. This is a way of life; I encourage you to get connected with someone who will guide you. Yes, a spiritual confidant. Join the church that best serves you and clear out the noise and be prepared to be transformed. Look, it's not the church that will give you peace. It's your ability to forgive, repent and be obedient. Do you think you can do that? Are you willing to submit?

Chapter 13:

Baptism

- Is baptism necessary?
- Why is baptism an essential component of your walk with Christ?
- What happens to your spirit the moment you enter the blessed water?

I was about 39 years old when I was baptized for the second time in my life. It happened about 6:30 a.m. in the warm waters of Deerfield Beach, Florida. This was a unique and memorable experience in my life because for the first time I became part of something real, meaningful, majestic and extraordinary. I became a member of the new covenant and was overcome with a sense of peace and joy. There was an extraordinary sensation and powerful burning on my chest. It was a glorious moment.

In the New Testament we find various chapters and verses on baptism in Luke, John, Acts, Matthew, Colossians, Romans, 1 Peter, Mark, Ephesians, and Revelation. In Christianity, the word baptism comes from the Greek "baptizo," meaning submerged, dipped in, plunged. It is a ritual whereby an individual, depending upon the Christian denomination, may enter into salvation and the community of believers of the faith.

Baptism is translated seventy six times in the New Testament. Why is baptism a central theme in the Gospels? How did it impact the teachings of Christ? In what way does baptism symbolize a new beginning? What role did John the Baptist play according to the scriptures? Does baptism pave the way to salvation?

Christian water baptism means submitting to the will of God and His righteousness, leaving behind the lust, envy and other lures of the world. The act of baptism, when done in faith, introduces the believer to a world filled with blessings. The decision to be baptized is a serious one and so much more relevant in today's society when most are going through some type of affliction and looking for a quick fix.

In Romans 6:3-7, the apostle Paul gives us insight about the kind of worldly substance that is left behind and what is gained through faith:

"Faith and know ye not that so many of us as were baptized into Jesus Christ were baptized into his death? Therefore we are buried with him by baptism into death: that like as Christ was raised up from the dead by the glory of the Father, even so we also should walk in newness of life. For if we have been planted together in the likeness of his death, we shall be also in the likeness of his resurrection:

Knowing this, that our old man is crucified with him, that the body of sin might be destroyed, that henceforth we should not serve sin. For he that is dead is freed from sin allows for the Holy Spirit to operate and because of it your soul is saved."

BAPTISM'S SYMBOLISM

In the Christian faith there are three baptisms for believers - repentance, water baptism and Holy Spirit baptism. The Holy Spirit, always present and active, engages the mind and soul of humanity. Water is symbolically the source of life, crucial to our existence. It is through this medium that the Holy Spirit navigates and consuls the soul, attitude and mindset of those who remain in constant alertness and are willing to live in love, joy and compassion. Water baptism is, in fact, the culminating seal, as found in the Gospel of John 3:13-15. In this chapter, Jesus directs John the Baptist to fulfill the prophecy by being immersed in the river Jordan.

It is the belief of the Christian faith that baptism washes away all sins and permits the Holy Spirit to spring into action in the name of Jesus Christ. After reading several verses in the Book of Acts, I was struck by Acts 2:3 a remarkable message. There was one of those "aha" moments for me. Think about it for a minute. Are we worthy of receiving the Holy Spirit?

I think of the daily struggles and the areas where God is working on me and my convictions and working in my spiritual journey. In essence, without my obedience, how can the mysteries of the Gospels come to life and the Word of God be revealed?

Baptism represents the metamorphosis of the physical (mind, emotions, memories) and spiritual awakening of humanity, for in it there is a transformation. As you continue on this journey, I am also walking that road with you. Your spiritual development is a decision and way of life. We pray and await answers in obedience without being jolted to act on impulse.

Folks, I haven't spoken to you about prayer because I had to set the stage. In the following chapter, I will expand further on how prayer changed my life.

Chapter 14:

A Son's Question: The Power of Prayer

- Does prayer work?
- Is there a way to pray?
- How do we know God is listening?
- Did Christ provide a model for us to use?

PRAYERS OPEN THE GATEWAY TO HEAVEN

Prayer has allowed me to search deep within my soul for unfound answers as to why it hurts so much to witness the self-destructive nature of humanity.

Several years ago, I had a rough day at work and vented for a while with my son who was 20 years old at the time. He said, "Dad, why do you care so much? It's difficult to change some of these teenagers." I had to think for a minute to respond in a way where I could reach his soul. You see, my son was also going through a spiritual renewal himself. He, too, was in search of answers. My prayer then and now continues to be that he may find answers in the spirit and not in logic.

As a school leader, I realize there are days when work is daunting, drawing us inward and at times we may even feel overwhelmed due to transference. Inevitably it happens. How can we avoid not being affected? How can you just disconnect and not be moved by human affliction?

I believe that resiliency, faith and the Holy Spirit have and will continue to bring peace and strength regardless of the circumstances we are exposed to in the work place. The school setting is the bubble that captures all the inequities of the secular world. It is a place where all afflictions are in competition, exposing the cruel nature of the evil one.

The presence of prayer is what inoculates the environment, trust me. I continue to pray for those souls who are in anguish and have no way of getting to the Bridge of Righteousness I have referred to in previous chapters.

My son's statement about caring made me reflect. I realized that there was much more behind this comment.

THE BRAIN AND PRAYER

I searched and found several scholarly journals that made mention of the brain and the power of prayer and came across one particular article of interest. For instance, researchers at the University of Massachusetts and Harvard Neurological

Departments have concluded that prayers can alter the brain.

"The analysis of modern science now confirms that a person's developed quality of compassion can have measured physical effects. According to Richard Davidson, director of the Laboratory for Affective Neuroscience at Harvard, these are "virtuous qualities…skills of the mind which can be developed through certain practices because of the plasticity of the brain." Prayer can literally change our brain (Berger, p.17).

Similarly, the world of biomedicine is witnessing an amazing transformation as attitudes about spirituality in the world of medicine are beginning to redefine how physicians are treating their patients and science is re-developing a partnership with spirituality built on the premise of faith.

Researchers have found, "There [is a growing sense of discovery] in both the religious and medical worlds, that 'prayer is good medicine' and religion is good for your health," (Epperly, p.26). This study reveals that people who are active in the church are less likely to suffer long term illness and heart disease, particularly in Seventh Day Adventist and Church of Latter Day Saints.

PRAYER: A STATE OF MIND

Prayers to consider when in need:

The Lord's Prayer is the foundation of all prayers, modeled by Jesus Christ. We look at such things as praising, giving thanks despite circumstances and events, intercession, etc. I am reminded of message of Proverbs 23:7: "Will a man's thought provoke who he is to become?"

The study on prayer goes on to mention that personal beliefs have altered the degree and impact of the ailment as a result of the patient's mood or [aggressive pursuit] of healing."Loneliness, guilt, hopelessness, stress and isolation have been identified as having a causal influence in the occurrence of cancer and heart disease. While once feelings, attitudes, and beliefs were dismissed as insignificant factors in medical evidence and practice, a wider empirism is emerging in the edges of biomedicine which recognizes the significance of non-sensory experiences, personal beliefs and spiritual practices along with the empirical findings of C-T Scans, MRIs, Blood Work ups, and EEGs as legitimate sources of medical evidence (p.24).

Prayer operates in the arena of faith and under the guidance of the Holy Spirit in forging a forgiving heart. We see it in Hebrews 11:6, Jude: 20, and Mark 11:25-26.

Understanding God's will in your life requires you to have a genuine relationship with the Father. This means fasting, praying and spending intimate moments with Christ. How can we determine what God wants from us and how can we remain honest, truthful, joyful and prudent in our behavior and attitudes?

What does Colossians 1:9 tell us, as believers? We need to be filled with wisdom and spiritual understanding at all times.

When we are taken from glory to glory, there is an alignment of conduct that surpasses all logic. How can we determine if God will approve? Consider a person's state of mind and spiritual awareness. Only when something is proven to be good, acceptable and perfect will we know that the grace of God is with us. For instance, look at a child's smile and the way in which that child hugs those most precious around them. Similarly, what about the birth of a child? These moments are imprinted in your mind forever. The Word of God endures forever (Isaiah 40:8).

FAREWELL PRAYERS

A closing prayer tells us that whatsoever we ask in the name of Christ, we shall receive because of faith. Man was created in the image of God; Christ suffered, died and was resurrected on the third day. What does this mean to those who believe? The Lord made us rulers and ambassadors of the Kingdom and, as such, we have power that when two or more seek His presence, agree and ask for the purpose of His will, all things become real. Prayer cultivates another righteous passageway into Eden. It is through prayer that we may see the true manifestation of the Holy Spirit on earth.

During your walk in faith be aware. The constant trials and tribulations are a mark of the evil one. But you are holy - consecrated to do good things. Do not be overwhelmed; stay focused. In prayer, much will be revealed so that you may be comforted and strengthened like Paul while he was imprisoned. Had Paul not been jailed, would we have the benefits and blessings of the Epistles? These trials, the constant attacks, build character in Christ Jesus. Blaming God for obstacles is not an option folks. Now, what is it that God wants from us?

Chapter 15:

A Father's Wish

- When considering a father's wish for his children, what are the thoughts that activate memories of great fortune or misfortune?
- Are fathers not worried about their children's future?

In today's society, humanity is absorbed with individualities and unfortunate economic woes. Equally as important, however, is the idea that we have been created in the image of the Almighty God. Why is it so challenging to do His will? Calamities, compounded by lost identity and purpose, can often blind us and wealth - or the love of it - cannot redeem or save us.

From the inception of time, the Lord established the law and identified unique individuals to fulfill their destiny and provide for those in need. By perfect design and in Christ Jesus we may be permitted to partake in that joyous journey and answer the question: What is God's will for us?

The will of God is seen in Matthew 6:33 (KJV): "But seek ye first the kingdom of God, and His righteousness; and all these things shall be added unto you."

It's a matter of having a relationship with the Creator, not a ritual or a "have to do" experience. It is a desire to be obedient so that the soul, mind and spirit may always be in the grace and glory of Christ Jesus. May man receive the revelation that in Christ Jesus we find a greater wealth through the mysteries of the Gospels.

GOD'S WISH

God has a goal for humanity and it may be forged as a result of our unique ability to have a relationship with Him. There are five very essential blessings: spiritual, physical healing, ***Prosperity, economic prosperity and redemption**. In Ephesians 1:3-1 we discover what the spiritual blessings of the believer are, how God gives those blessings and the reasons why we may partake in them. Through Christ Jesus, we are adopted sons and have redemption. We forgive our trespassers and know the mystery of His will. We have obtained an inheritance, and most importantly, we are sealed with the Holy Spirit.

In essence, the seal preserves us; we are constantly redeemed in the blood of Christ because He intercedes on our behalf to the Father. Through the Grace of the Lord, humanity is sanctified and saved. By walking in truth through Jesus, our Spirit is a lamp of light in the eyes of our Lord God. That is the reason why I call us the "Bridged Ones." I have often found a sense of relief when I turn to Psalms. David has a unique way of connecting the reader to God by placing our thoughts and focal point toward heaven. Your walk with God will enable you to speak to Him in the same way David did thousands of years ago. Our faith is strengthened when we see God's hands at work. I am referring to the way we respond to moments of grief and despair in the same manner David was confronted.

Let us further examine physical health, healing and prosperity. Psalms 91:1-3 (KJV) says: "He that dwelleth in the secret place of the most High shall abide under the shadow of the Almighty. I will say of the Lord, He is my refuge and fortress. My God; in Him will I trust. Surely He shall deliver thee from the snare of the fowler; and from the noisome pestilence." (KJV)

God's will for humanity is a common theme that can be found in both the Old and New Testaments. In Psalms 91, I find great delight knowing that I can and will reside in the shadow (presence) and glory of God. It is not just a catchy verse; it is a verse of fortitude and unyielding trust and confidence.

Christ was crucified and nailed on the cross for our transgressions (sins), so that each time He was stricken we may receive eternal salvation and deliverance from the inner crater of the abyss.

Is there a void in your life now? If so, how do you compensate? What does it mean to live an abundant life and how will it impact future generations? Is there a connection between physical needs and spiritual needs?

We know that Christ came, died and was risen so that we may have an abundant life. A person's lifestyle, decisions and ability to live a full life rests on obedience and acknowledgement of the significance of the scriptures.

Creating a balance of spirituality requires a truthful heart and willingness to activate the Word, and through the Word we are freed. Achieving a victorious lifestyle as a Christian requires an in-depth look at the physical and the spiritual needs of humanity.

WHAT IS IT THAT YOU NEED?

In Maslow's hierarchy of needs, at the very top of the pyramid we find the realization of goals, dreams and authenticity. In the absence of Christ, humanity lives by instincts. As Christians, however, we live in the presence of praising the Lord and being thankful for all our experiences. David was inspired and motivated in Psalms 29:2 (KJV): "...Worship the Lord in the beauty of Holiness."

Through faith and discerning the Word we can repel the darts of Satan and through the testimony of events, we rejoice in our attempts to live a righteous life in the eyes of our Lord Jesus Christ.

Love fills a void. It lifts, embraces and strengthens us so that we may reach an everlasting dimension of hope and joy through Christ Jesus. In the absence of love there is chaos, animosity and the complete destruction of humanity as evident in the thousands of years of world wars as humanity has evolved.

LOVE MOVES US

Did Abraham love God? Did Noah intercede because he loved humanity? Was Moses simply inspired by compassion or was he moved by love? God is love and through Him we find an everlasting promise. There is no compromise for the true covenant that comes through a daily talk with the Lord. Each of these biblical characters was a "victor." They overcame adversity and their testimonies have been inspirational to countless generations.

In Christ, we find ourselves victorious and guided by the fruits of the Spirit as it is written in Galatians 5:22-23. As we mature in the faith, praise, fast, and pray. We are given the unique opportunity to stand before Christ and know that we are consecrated to fulfill a divine purpose. It is an honor and privilege to write about the very thing that we continue to battle each day of our lives. Paul tells us in Galatians 5:16-18 that the battle is all in the mind, in the spirit and in our ability to draw strength from the Gospels. We must do the will of God, remain in constant prayer and give thanks at all times. A carnal mind leads to death and a spiritual mind washes away those nightmares which, in turn, bring peace and an end to the enslavement to memories. What is the wish of a relentless, loving father? I believe that is to have his children prepared and anointed for the battle.

As Christians, we must be vigilant and recognize the mechanisms the devil plots, designs and orchestrates in an effort to penetrate our souls, minds and spirits.

I submit to Christ and acknowledge my trust in Him above all things seen and unseen in the eyes of man. The path to righteousness is a lonely one but our victory is secured for the Lord, too, was tempted in the flesh and we hope that we may find mercy through His grace and glory.

For that reason, I pray that I may continue to remain in the Spirit, walk in the steps of Christ, have the mind of Christ and be the voice of Christ in trying times.

Living an abundant life requires only a genuine relationship with Christ. Yes, I understand that in life I have physical needs and spiritual needs and that there is a constant battle in the flesh. But, I choose Christ as my healer and defender and, as such, all my trust is in Him.

Chapter 16:

Temptation

- What is it about temptation that lures us away from the light?
- How has temptation affected humanity since the first man sinned?
- How can you fight temptation in the midst of so much influence?
- How did Christ deal with it?

We all face temptation every single day. How and when you deal with it is a testimony between you and God. Let me tell you something folks, God does not tempt us. Listen, would you consider the way in which the devil tempted Christ as He was confronted in the desert for forty days? The devil knew Jesus. Imagine how clever he is. He even tempted Christ. Can you imagine what he is doing in the world today? Look around in your communities, in the city, in the news. When have you ever heard good news? Please don't mistake my analogy here. I am only suggesting that, as Christians, we remain anchored in faith and not on the calamities we witness on a daily basis through social media. How often have you declared a word of salvation onto those who seemed overwhelmed by their current problems at home or at work or who faced serious financial and health issues?

Jesus called upon scripture over and over again in Luke 4:1-4. This is how he demonstrated His authority over all principalities. Yes, temptations are governed by these, but in Christ, in praising, in fellowship, in prayer we break out. We are freed from slavery, from the type of temptations that have broken homes and lured humanity to the brink of chronic depression and ultimately to suicide.

Temptation plays a vital role in the formation of the human spirit through trials and the unyielding manifestation of uncontrolled behavior. Temptation is often seen as negative but it can be positive as well.

Six years ago, I was aggressively pursuing a promotion. I did everything I thought was right. Guess what? I was given an opportunity to interview with a panel, was highly recommended and figured I was in for sure. I didn't receive a call, I can tell you I was so disappointed that I even considered switching careers. I was disappointed and had no sense of direction until one day someone suggested I apply for this position in another county. I guess the Lord had other plans for me. It's been three years since I received the promotion to work full time in alternative education. I have been truly blessed. So you see, despite my eagerness to get promoted and get an ego boost, God was working in me.

I am now working with the same kids I was referring to at an alternative site as a school administrator. Is God not amazing? I was struggling to get a promotion when, all along, God had reserved a position for me somewhere else. Listen, I prayed every single day for guidance and in the decision I was about to make. These interviews took me around the country, from Orlando to Philadelphia, to Tennessee. Who would have imagined that? I love airplane rides and yes, the Lord protected me along the way.

As Christians we will inevitably be tempted. The question is how will we respond to that temptation and will we hold fast and trust in the inner voice of the Holy Spirit for continual guidance? Overcoming temptation is an-ongoing battle and recognizing the mechanism used by the devil can be easily revealed through the Holy Scriptures.

The purpose of temptation is to get us to deviate from God's plan and His will on earth. Temptation begins in the heart and leads to the mind which ultimately leads to the flesh. In 1 John 2:16 we get better clarity:

"For all that is in the world—the lust of the flesh, the lust of the eyes, and the pride of life—is not of the Father but is of the world." (NIV)

These temptations were first used by Satan on Adam and Eve and are clearly present in our life today - most evident in and delivered through media and on-line sources. Consider most of the popular TV shows and media blogs which have been carefully crafted and timed to impact a targeted audience - our youth today. I am not bashing or judging. I am making the point that these are platforms that are used to sell an idea and these ideas spread and consume the world.

I make a reference to this in the context of 1 Peter 5:8 because I want to remind you of what the darkness is like. It is like a roaring lion looking to devour our souls. Is this not evident in the quasi-pornographic visuals we see in today's music videos? It hurts to see so many of our children lost and it is up to us to create meaningful programs that will transform these tempted minds and hearts.

From its inception, as we consider Genesis 3:5-6, the law had been established - and yet temptation continually leads us to disobedience.

As Christians we need to think about the battle and be prepared, willing and able to confront Satan. Paul goes into great detail in Ephesians 6:11 and 13-17 explaining how we can move forward in the Spirit. Christ was tempted in the wilderness three times and each time he dismantled the devil's sting by proclaiming the Word. We must stay tuned to the daily verses, commit them to memory, and study them, for they will keep you guarded and bring everlasting life (Matthew 4:1-11).

Can you imagine Satan's craftiness? If he was given carte-blanche to tempt Christ, how much more damage can he do to man? Although at times we may feel as if the whole world is caving in. We find rescue - a window of escape, a bridge to cross - in Christ our Lord. We are connected to the Father. It's a matter of resisting the devil and proclaiming our inheritance in the heavens with Christ as our brother and our sustainer.

In the event I sin, I repent and re-establish my relationship with the Father. The devil will attempt to hold me hostage, imposing guilt, remorse and accusation on me for the sin. But, I can dismiss the devil's accusations and reclaim my righteous path with Christ.

Think about your relationship with the Lord. How often do you pray? Are you fasting, praising and reading the Bible? In order to combat temptation, you must identify the source, apply discernment and give it little credit. It does not mean that you do not give temptation importance; instead, it is just a matter of creating a balance.

When asked by friends and family members how I am able to create that balance of peace, I say this: When in doubt, look at Proverbs for guidance and when in need of fortification and strength, consider the Psalmist David, particularly Psalms 23. The most important thing to do when confronted by sin is to recognize the disobedience, speak to the Lord and ask for forgiveness. At best, run away from the situation (temptation) like Joseph did when he resisted Potiphar's wife (Genesis 39:6-12).

AWARENESS

There are seven stages to be aware of in the process of succumbing to sin:

- Imagination - What is it that you are feeding the mind?

- Lust (Desire) - How often are you on-line surfing for pornography?
- Enticement - Where does it begin and how do you disconnect?
- Temptation - Who is in control?
- Sin - Is it real?
- Death (the actual sin) - How far from God are you in this journey?

I think of temptation as the platform of choice to disconnect humanity from righteousness. It is an arena where we, as gladiators welded in faith, must receive our freedom from the "kills" (when temptations are laid to rest) which will ultimately send us to that next dimension of being an overcomer - known as glory.

Today I am a forty five year old man expressing a thought, an idea that perhaps may transform your mind. I have evolved and was not always as anchored in faith as I am today. I am very humble and thankful for bringing together these thoughts into your life. It is my prayer that you may find the mind and body of Christ in scripture and that it alters your heart and soul. My other prayer is that you never give up.

May I remind you that there is something much bigger in your life. You have purpose. You are dearly loved and protected by the Arch Angels. You have much to think about in the next days, weeks and months. Search deep within you and reflect on Scripture. You are not alone. Go and find your divine, sacred purpose: only you can decide in what direction to go. Remember, you have will power; this power cannot be taken away from you. It was intended to fulfill a prophecy. The crown of righteousness is your shadow. Like me, see yourself as an overcomer. The crown of righteousness is ours to wear!

A Final Prayer

I have decided to welcome the idea of mission work. I have joined a wonderful church family that truly embodies the love of Christ on earth. I am filled with their guidance, love and support. Moving forward, I intend to join an advanced discipleship course and serve in Youth Ministry around our community in West Palm Beach, Florida.

My children are all in their 20s now, I recently became a grandfather and then my oldest announced that she, too, is pregnant. Imagine that - two grandchildren in one year. WOW. I work with at risk children and feel the love of Christ in the work that we do in changing the mind-set of failure into success as many are graduating from high school and pursuing postsecondary education.

I am exploring the idea of traveling overseas to Central and South America and speaking to the young men and women who have been forgotten. Society calls them misfits; I call them the blessed ones. These kids (16-21) have lost hope and have not experienced love in a long time. This project of traveling and evangelizing has been burning in my heart for many years. I will prepare for this journey with the help of my new-found family, my church. I am guided by the spirit and I will obey. This is where I stand today, my friends. All these degrees and titles mean nothing if I can't give back. I will serve with joy - and why not? I was homeless, hungry, angry, humiliated, desperate, tempted and depressed but I never stopped being connected to God, not even at a young age. The Lord saw me through it all, His mercy shielded me.

Today I am at peace with God's presence in my life. I value and treasure where I stand anchored in faith. I am sharing my story because I know that many of you out there are struggling the same way I did when I dropped out of school. When I thought I couldn't handle life's punches, I reconnected with Christ. He was always present. Folks, this is about faith. This is about never giving up.

Now, I rest on the shoulders of the Lord. I am not afraid of the future and what it holds for me for I am saved in the blood of Christ. I begin a new phase of my life filled with great anticipation as I submit to the will of God.

I confess my sins - for they are many - but I desire to serve and so I declare the prayer of faith. This new journey will take me to new places to see the plight of humanity firsthand as a missionary, evangelist and author.

I'm in a different place today because your Word sustains and comforts me. It moves me into the supernatural. The old Victor is dead (the one that tried to make it on his own without having Christ set as first priority), thank goodness. I have a sense of relief after this long-fought journey. The battle has been constant and yet you have never abandoned me. You are mighty, my Lord. Join me in prayer as I enter the temple where He dwells.

I find strength in your Psalms and knowledge in your Proverbs. I am no longer disgusted with life. Your presence and promises follow me; they act as wings on my feet. Man has offended you and so have I. Forgive me Father. I repent and I long to stay within your presence and grace, Jehovah.

Father, countless have been the moments where the attacks of the enemy have blemished my sight, but through your everlasting Word have I lived. Thank you Christ, for by your blood I am healed. There will no longer be thoughts of despair in me. I cancel all things, all principalities and all calculated schemes that come against your anointed one, oh Father - against all authorities - and I bind them in the name of Christ.

I am clear about whom I serve and about my purpose. It is to serve you Lord, to keep constantly connected to thy righteousness. Thy Word shall be my shield all day. Your grace is in me and I am in you. I choose you and your will and have a heightened awareness. Today, I am clear. I have your sight. I will speak your language and walk in faith. I shall walk the unsafe waters in your name and I will be triumphant.

I have discovered the clues and roots of evil – they were subtle at first, but now I recognize Him. I stand firm in you, Father, for thy sword will do battle in your name. I shall wear the helmet of salvation and breastplate of righteousness. I will no longer go to battle without your armor.

As I look back on past experiences, the decisions I made without your approval planted seeds of doubt in me. Now, your light shall pave the way for me and may I never again walk in darkness. Brothers and sisters, please pray for the saints. I leave you with one final verse - Corinthians 2:15-17:

"The spiritual man makes judgments about all things, but he himself is not subject to any man's judgment: For who has known the mind of the Lord that he may instruct him? But we have the mind of Christ."

The road to recovery - to overcoming feelings of helplessness and despair, experiences of confusion and loneliness, and negative memories that have kept us bound - begins when I acknowledge the strength and presence of Christ on the cross. I now also understand that this cross may bring you to the road of salvation and eternal life.

No other book in the history of humanity will ever make a greater impact than the Bible. I pray that you may rest and find peace in the death and resurrection of the new you in the body of Christ.

I leave you in peace and pray for you always.

Amen!

Made in United States
North Haven, CT
30 October 2021

10697186R00066